NATURAL WONDERS

BY TONY HARVEY

CONTENTS

(*Left*) Red Canyon, Utah, USA. The sculpted rocks and exotic colouring combine to create a very distinctive landscape.

INTRODUCTION

The earth's grandest illusion is that it appears never to change; a myth which has become embodied in our everyday language. 'As old as the hills', 'the everlasting sea', '*terra firma*' all embody the concept of a never-changing earth. True there are occasional dramatic and often devastating volcanic eruptions and earthquakes, but such events only ever affect a relatively small area of the earth's surface.

The earth's secret is time. Spans of time which are measured not in hundreds of years, but in hundreds of thousands and millions of years. The most important agent in the moulding of the earth is water. Water, time and gravity together can achieve the impossible.

As rain falls on the earth's surface, some of this weakly-acidic liquid eats its way into the rocks, gradually gouging out cracks and crevices. Percolating underground, it continues its work to create caves and caverns of immense size. Some of the rain runs directly off the surface into streams which unite to form mighty rivers thousands of miles long.

Rivers are constantly eroding their own courses, removing vast quantities of rocks and sediment. In the upland areas, the main activity is directed

The earth is full of contrasts. Below majestic waves, ideal for surfing, break on a Hawaiian shore. On the right is Mount Ama Dhablam in Nepal, one of the majestic peaks of the Himalayas.

to cutting downwards, creating steep-sided valleys which swing to and fro between interlocking spurs of land.

Where tough outcrops of rock are encountered rapids and waterfalls develop. Lower down its course, the river concentrates on widening its valley, depositing some of its load. It meanders from side to side. When it reaches the sea, its load of rocks and sediment either builds up at its mouth to form a delta, or is swept out to sea by the currents.

The water in the oceans is constantly attacking the shoreline, driven on to greater feats by the tides and storms. In many places cliffs are being worn away at a considerable pace, endangering homes, while the products of such destruction are being deposited elsewhere to create new areas of land.

Not all the water which reaches the earth's surface does so as rain; some arrives as fog, hail or snow. In the high mountains, and in the polar regions, snow may remain from year to year, gradually becoming packed into ice which will eventually flow like a river down the valleys as a glacier. It is only 12,000 years since the last ice sheets retreated from northern Europe.

Much of the scenery of the northern world owes its appearance to the work of ice. Amongst the most notable features are the U-shaped valleys and the great heaps of debris, called moraine, which mark pauses in the advance or retreat of a glacier.

Even without forming rivers of ice, water, when frozen, is a potent destroyer of the toughest rocks. In winter when it freezes in the cracks and crevices it expands, breaking off fragments continually.

It is not only on the surface of the earth that there is continual change; beneath lurk the immense forces of vulcanism. Many areas of the world are subjected to regular outbursts of volcanic activity, with great quantities of lava pouring out over the surface. Occasionally whole islands may be blown apart by a single volcanic eruption, while on other occasions the out-pourings of lava can build a new land. Often associated with volcanic activity are the hot springs, spurting geysers and pools of boiling mud.

It is difficult to believe that the rocks which make

up the Himalayas were once sediments at the bottom of an ocean, but such is the way of the world. Once the Scottish Highlands and the Appalachian Mountains of the USA were as lofty as the Alps, but time changes all. There have been several periods of mountain building during the millions of years of earth history. All have taken their time, however, for it takes 10,000,000 years to build a mountain range.

But there are even greater forces at work, for 250 million years ago the distribution of land and sea was completely different from that of today.

Moab Deadhouse, Utah, (*right*) one of the magnificent canyons of the western USA, testifies to the effectiveness of water in shaping the landscape.

At that time one great land mass, called 'Pangaea', existed. Over millions of years this has gradually separated and split, until the land masses assumed their present shape.

The climate of the earth has also varied over the years. At present we are either at the end of an ice age, or in an inter-glacial period after which the ice sheets will return. Nor is the recent ice age the only period of severe climate which the earth has had to endure, for others have occurred several times before, approximately 940, 770, 615, 400 and 295 million years ago. For millions of years there were no ice sheets at all, and the earth as a whole experienced a more equable climate than at present.

It must not be assumed that the earth has stopped changing, for the continents are still drifting, some oceans are expanding and others contracting, water still moulds the surface and life continues to evolve.

Many of the most majestic scenes are in reality the remnants of former landscapes, for all the wonders illustrated in this book are but pauses in the long and ever-changing history of our planet.

WONDERS OF THE EARTH

Everywhere the earth's surface is decomposing and
disintegrating as the result of erosion. These processes
can give rise to spectacular shapes. In this photograph are the
Wetterhorn, Schreckhorn and Eiger peaks in the Swiss Alps.

Deserts and dunes

About one-fifth of the earth's surface is desert. The main deserts of the world are in central Asia, which includes the Gobi, in Africa – the Sahara and Kalahari deserts – in western Australia and in parts of western USA and South America.

There are two main types of sand dune: the seif, which is long and narrow, and the more attractive crescent-shaped barchan. Barchans are formed where the wind is constant; they have a gentle slope to windward, and a steep leeward slope. They move in the direction of the peaks, and can occur in isolation or in swarms. Sometimes they merge together as at Beni-Abbès, Algeria (*right*).

Monuments in rock

The wreck of former worlds by the action of water and wind is no more clearly shown than in parts of the western USA, and particularly in Monument Valley, Arizona (*right*). There rain, in the form of torrential downpours, has attacked the horizontally bedded strata, rapidly eroding the shales under the massive sandstones. Vast areas of rock have been removed. Where the capping rocks have proved particularly resistant they remain as isolated hills, which are often flat-topped, steep-sided and called mesas (or, if smaller, buttes).

Cathedral Gorge in Nevada (*below*) shows the effects of a similar climate on a very different type of rock. Clays (which formed on the floor of an ancient lake) have been eroded into draped spires reminiscent of cathedral architecture. Many land forms have distinctive shapes reflecting the processes by which they were moulded. No one agent of erosion works alone; all scenery is the result of features formed in a variety of ways. Climatic features such as the amount and seasonal distribution of rain and snow, temperature ranges, and wind strength and direction control the erosive processes of a particular region. Erosion works rapidly in steep areas with heavy precipitation, and in semi-arid areas with little vegetation.

Natural bridges

Differential weathering occurs where rocks with different resistance to the elements are found out-cropping together. The more resistant rocks are left, while the less resistant are eroded away. Some of the most attractive scenic features produced by such action are natural bridges and arches.

The Colorado Plateau of the western USA has a remarkable number of such monuments created by the action of the weather, and boasts one national park and two national monuments for their protection.

Skyline Arch, in Arches National Monument, Utah, USA (*above*), is just one of more than 100 arches in all stages of evolution and decay in the park. One of these, Landscape Arch, is 89m (291ft) long but only 3.3m (10.8ft) thick. All such arches originate by a process called 'holing'. Within an outcrop of rock, a less resistant layer is attacked by rain and wind, eventually creating a 'window'. Once formed, it continues to be enlarged, the weaker material

being removed leaving the stronger rock as the arch.

Natural bridges have a different origin. They result from changes in the course of a river. Owachomo Bridge, in the Natural Bridges National Monument of Utah, USA (*above*), is 55m (180ft) long and only 2.7m (6.7ft) thick. It is in the 'old-age' stage. Such bridges develop when a river which has created a large meander cuts through the neck of the peninsula of land

at the base of the meander. A bridge is formed, and the original 'U' shape of the river course is abandoned.

Also in Utah is the Rainbow Bridge, described as 'the most perfect natural bridge in the world'. Differential weathering of rocks can also create such bizarre forms as the block of 320 million-year-old millstone grit. This block is known as the Druid's Idol and can be found in Yorkshire, England (*far left*).

Underground worlds

Even below the deserts there is water somewhere, if you dig deep enough. The upper level of this ground water, as it is called, is the water-table. When a shaft is sunk, and the water-table is penetrated, the bore will immediately fill up with water.

In areas of limestone rock, rainwater, which is always slightly acidic due to the carbon dioxide dissolved in it, acts on the calcium carbonate of the rock. The rock is quite rapidly dissolved, and removed as calcium bicarbonate.

The water will gradually find its way into rock joints, going on downwards until it meets an impervious layer. It will seek a way out again at this lower level, which is sometimes many kilometres from where it first went underground. Once such an underground drainage system has been established, the river will continue to develop an intricate system of passages, sometimes many kilometres long. Some of the passages become enlarged to form caves and caverns. The limestone regions of the world are well known for their disappearing rivers, underground streams and caverns. There are large cave systems in the United States, the Alps and Pyrenees, south Australia, south China, Japan – Shuho-do Cave, Yamaguchi (*left*) – and Rumania – Meziad Cave, Bez (*above*).

Petrified waterfalls

Many cave systems present a wonderland of rushing streams, sparkling waterfalls and deep, still pools. Everywhere the lime-laden water is moulding the characteristic decorations of this underground world.

Drops of water on the ceiling leave behind deposits of lime as they fall. These gradually grow into a variety of shapes – large or small, solid and transparent – known as stalactites. The columns which grow upwards by the same process, are usually thicker. They are called stalagmites.

Sometimes the two join to form a pillar, or in other instances there are whole clusters which resemble the pipes of a cathedral organ.

Water continuously trickling from a roof fissure will gradually build a fluted formation like a curtain, while water running down a slope will create a petrified waterfall.

Speleologists, as those interested in the science of caves are known, have discovered a great deal about the geology and biology of these extremely dark, and seemingly inhospitable environments.

Also from caves have come important fossil finds of animals long extinct, for example, the cave bear. Perhaps most important of all, they have been a rich source for the remains of prehistoric man, whose first home was in caves.

(*Top left*) stalactites in the Castellana Grotto, Italy. (*Bottom left*) stalactites in Eberstadt, Germany. (*Above*) spectacular stalactites in in Czechoslovakia, near the Hungarian border.

Isolated hills

The earth's surface is under constant attack from the elements. The tendency is for even the highest mountain chain to be worn down completely to a flat surface, although such a condition is never reached.

In arid and semi-arid areas, the wearing down of hills and the retreat of the slopes tends to leave behind a gently sloping surface. Rising dramatically from such a plain are the isolated hills (called inselbergs) of which Ayers Rock, 483km (300m) south-west of Alice Springs, in the very heart of Australia, is a prime example (*below*). Ayers Rock, over 300m (1000ft) tall, is made up of Precambrian rocks which have been so contorted that they are now vertical. Although it appears from a distance as a regular dome, on closer inspection its surface is seen to bear many scars and gullies.

A similar residual hill which has formed in a tropical climate is Pão de Assucar, or the Sugar Loaf, which towers above the city of Rio de Janeiro, Brazil (*right*).

The Grand Canyon

There is no shortage of canyons and gorges in the river systems of the world, but without a doubt the most famous is that of the Colorado River, where it flows through the Grand Canyon. The Canyon is 349km (216m) long and in places is 2135m (6702ft) deep. The history of the river systems of the Colorado Plateau is complicated, but certainly commences with the building of the Rocky Mountains, 65 million years ago.

The formation of the inner Canyon is almost solely due to the river cutting into its bed, but in the wider parts of the Canyon (*below* and (*right*) rain and wind have also played quite a significant part in shaping the extraordinary steps and pinnacles. The oldest rocks of the walls are some 2000 million years old, and the exposed rocks present, in the words of the great American geologist and explorer John Wesley Powell (1834–1902), 'a book of revelations in the rock-leaved Bible of geology'.

Forests of stone

Petrified Forest National Park (*below* and *right*) in Arizona, USA, contains the fragments of thousands of fossilized trees.

There are several theories as to how so many trunks became fossilized together. One theory is that the trunks collected as a prehistoric log jam. They were overwhelmed by silt and sediment and, before the wood could rot, water saturated with minerals penetrated the logs. The minerals impregnated all the tissues and faithfully reproduced the bark, cells and growth rings.

FROM BENEATH THE EARTH'S CRUST

Aptly named after Vulcan, God of Fire, volcanoes are magnificent manifestations of the vast stores of energy which lie just below the earth's surface. Although their activity only affects a relatively small area, they have been held in awe throughout man's existence, and have become widely mythologized in folklore. Heimaey, one of the Westmann Islands to the south of Iceland, is entirely volcanic in origin. For 5000 years it had remained peaceful, until one morning in January 1973 when molten lava spurted forth. Within three weeks the volcanic cone in this picture, about 200m (650ft) high, had built up.

Fire from the earth

During the earth's long history, most parts of its surface have witnessed some form of volcanic activity. A volcano is a point on the earth's surface from which volcanic material pours forth. More usually it is associated with a cone-shaped hill, made up of rock debris, solidified lava and ash, which is gradually built up around the initial vent.

Although volcanoes are found throughout the world, they are confined to areas of weakness in the earth's crust. These include the 'ring of fire' around the Pacific Ocean, The East African Rift Valley, and the Mediterranean.

Each volcanic eruption has its own character, but certain similarities can be recognized. The Hawaiian type of eruption, typified by the volcanoes of the Hawaiian Islands, spreads basaltic lava over a wide area. At the summits of such volcanoes there are lava lakes (*left* and *below*'.

The regular type of eruption of, for instance, Stromboli, north of Sicily, has earned it the title 'lighthouse of the Mediterranean'. Volcanoes do not always destroy land and buildings as Vesuvius did. Often they create new land, such as the Island of Surtsey (*right*).

of the North Island of New Zealand are considered to have been the finest of all such deposits. Although they were destroyed by an earthquake in 1886, it is still possible to catch some of their glory. In the words of a pioneer of New Zealand geology: 'The outlet of the spring has built up a system of sinter terraces on the slope of the hill, which, white as if hewn from marble, afford a prospect which no description or illustration has power to reproduce. It is as if a waterfall plunging over steps had been suddenly transformed to stone.'

NATURE'S FACTS AND FIGURES

As grand and spectacular as the natural world undoubtedly is, man has often gone to considerable trouble to establish its records – the longest, the fastest, the oldest, the largest.

Several hundred thousand earthquakes occur each year, but only a few of these are strong enough to cause damage or loss of life.

The distribution of both volcanoes and earthquakes in the world is closely linked with zones of weakness in the earth's crust. The 'ring of fire' around the Pacific Ocean is well known, while other zones of volcanic activity stretch along the ocean ridges and the rift valleys (for example in East Africa). Another line passes through the Mediterranean and into the Middle East.

The Andes are dominated by volcanoes, and the Caribbean area is extremely active. Not all volcanoes build up their cones slowly. The record for the most rapid growth is held by Parícutin in Mexico which within five months built a cone 458m (1480 feet) tall.

Many volcanoes which have been long extinct form important features of the landscape. Particularly noticeable are the great lava plateaux:

Columbia Plateau (North America): 130,000sq.km.
Deccan Traps (India): 500,000sq.km.
Parana (South America): 750,000sq.km.

Volcanic necks are often prominent features too, for example the Shiprock, New Mexico, and in France.

Closely associated with volcanic activity are thermal springs (hot springs) and geysers. The best known of all the geysers is Old Faithful, in the Yellowstone National Park, USA, which regularly shoots water 45m (150 feet) into the air. For a short period at the beginning of this century a geyser in New Zealand regularly discharged water to a height of 500m (1640 feet).

The main regions in which hot springs are found are Iceland, North America and New Zealand, but many other areas also have examples.

The great mountain chains of the world form some of the earth's most majestic scenery. But they are not all the same age: for example, the Appalachians and the mountains of central Europe originated about 280 million years ago; the Rockies of North America are about 90 million years old, and the Himalayas and Alps, the youngest, are a mere 20 million years old.

Canyons, natural arches and bridges make striking landscapes, and many of the most famous are to be found in North America. The greatest canyon of all must be the Grand Canyon (average depth 1739m (5700 feet)) but even this is not the deepest, for Hells Canyon on the Snake River averages 2013m (6500 feet).

Water falls are fairly common in many areas, but are spectacular nevertheless. However, those with the largest fall rarely have the greatest flow, nor are they necessarily the widest. For example the Victoria Falls on the Zambezi River, East Africa, are more than 1.6km (1 mile) wide while 13,160 cubic metres of water per second pass over the Guaira Falls on the Paraná River. The world's most visited falls are the Niagara Falls, 763m (2500 feet) wide, and 49m (160 feet) high.

Water in the form of ice has shaped much of the landscape, and at the height of the last glaciation period covered 45,693,106sq.km. of the land. Today the largest areas of ice are in Greenland (217,503sq.km.) and Antarctica (12,999,987sq.km.).

It is in Asia that many of the major valley glaciers are located, but most of the high mountain ranges support some glaciers. The largest of these rivers of ice can reach for over 490km (304 miles).

Major Islands
Greenland: 2,175,600sq.km.
New Guinea: 821,030sq.km.
Borneo: 744,366sq.km
Malagasy: 590,002sq.km.
Baffin Island: 476,067sq.km.
Sumatra: 473,607sq.km.

Mountain Ranges
Andes: 7241km. long.
Rocky Mountains: 6034km. long.
Himalayas: 3862km. long.
Great Dividing Range (Australia): 3620km. long.
Antarctica: 3540km. long.
Alps: 1050km. long.

Deserts
Sahara (Africa): 8,417,500sq.km.
Australian Desert: 1,554,000sq.km.
Arabian Desert: 1,295,000sq.km.
Gobi Desert (China): 1,036,000sq.km.
Kalahari Desert (southern Africa): 518,000sq.km.

Oceans and Seas
Pacific Ocean: 165,384,000sq.km.
Atlantic Ocean: 82,217,000sq.km.
Indian Ocean: 73,481,000sq.km.
Arctic Ocean: 14,056,000sq.km.
Mediterranean Sea: 2,505,000sq.km.
Caribbean Sea: 1,942,500sq.km.
North Sea: 572,390sq.km.
Black Sea: 436,415sq.km.

Major Rivers
Nile (Africa): 7944km.
Amazon (South America): 6275km.
Mississippi-Missouri (North America): 6230km.
Yangtze (Asia): 5470km.
Zaire (Africa): 4666km.

Lena (Asia): 4601km.
Amur (Asia): 4505km.
Hwango Ho (Asia): 4344km.
Paraná (South America): 3943km.
Murray-Darling (Australia): 3701km.
Volga (Asia): 3690km.
Danube (Europe): 2848km.
Indus (Asia): 2736km.

Major Lakes
Caspian Sea (USSR/Iran): 393,898sq.km.
Superior (Canada/USA): 82,810sq.km.
Victoria (East Africa): 69,470sq.km.
Aral (USSR): 68,682sq.km.
Huron (Canada/USA): 59,580sq.km.
Michigan (USA): 57,900sq.km.
Tanganyika (East Africa): 32,890sq.km.
Great Bear (Canada): 31,792sq.km.
Baikal (USSR): 31,492sq.km.
Great Slave (Canada): 28,483sq.km.
Eyre (Australia): 9324sq.km.
Titicaca (South America): 9060sq.km.

Major Waterfalls
Angel Falls (Venezuela): 980m.
Cuquenan Falls (Venezuela): 608m.
Yosemite Falls (USA): 534m.
Gavarnie (France): 422m.
Tugela Falls (South Africa): 411m.
Gersoppa (India): 252m.

Major Volcanic Eruptions
1500 BC, Santorini, Aegean Sea: Destruction of the Minoan civilization.
AD72, Vesuvius, Italy: Destruction of Pompeii and Herculaneum.
1815, Tambora, Sumbawa, Java: 92,000 killed.
1883, Krakatoa, Java/Sumatra: 36,000 killed.
1902, Mont Pelée, Martinique: 30,000 killed.

WATERY WONDERS

Every minute 15,000,000 cubic feet of water weighing
417,000 tonnes plunge over the Niagara Falls, on the
Canada/USA frontier. On the Canadian side (*shown here*)
they have the characteristic horseshoe shape of waterfalls,
which has earned them the name Horseshoe Falls.

Giant waterfalls

Waterfalls, as attractive as they are scenic, are geologically short-lived. Their initial development depends on the type of rock over which the river flows. When a resistant layer of rock is followed by one which is easily eroded, the latter part of the river channel will be deepened more quickly. The result will be a waterfall where the two layers meet. At other times the great basaltic plateaux have been lifted slowly to give ideal conditions for the evolution of waterfalls; some of the world's most spectacular leaps are at such locations. For example the Guayra Falls on the Parana River, on the borders of Brazil and Paraguay, where there are 18 separate falls, although their average height is only 33m (108ft).

The highest fall in the world is the silk-like thread of the Angel Falls in Venezuela (*far right*), with a total fall of 979m (3211ft).

The roar of the Iguassú Falls (*centre*), on the border of Brazil and Argentina, can be heard many kilometres away. In reality there are hundreds of individual falls, separated by small islands resplendent with lush, tropical vegetation. The total width of the falls is about 4km (2.5 miles) and the average drop 64m (210ft).

Of all the sights on earth which tourists travel to see 'none is so beautiful, so glorious, or so powerful', wrote the novelist Anthony Trollope (1815–83) as the Niagara Falls (*far left*).

Winter landscapes

In many regions of the world, the end of summer means more than merely the leaves turning colour and falling and the onset of colder weather. It means that the once green landscape will soon be covered by a white mantle of snow. This white cloak will provide essential water and protection for the plants that it covers, but will cause havoc to human society and particularly to systems of transport.

Of course, many areas of the world are permanently covered with snow and ice. The snow-line is an imaginary line drawn on the earth's surface above which there is snow throughout the year. In the Himalayas and in Africa, the line varies between 5185m (17,000ft) and 5795m (18,000ft) above sea level, by the Alps it is down to 2745m (7000ft), in south Greenland it is 610m (2000ft) and towards the polar areas it is at sea-level. The highest peaks in the United Kingdom are just below the snow-line for the appropriate latitude, although

on Ben Nevis some snow does remain for most years in the north-facing gullies.

The very cold areas of the earth do not all have permanent snow or, indeed much snow at all; for example in Siberia the general level of precipitation is too low.

Snow may appear attractive once on the ground, but both its coming and its going can be violent and dangerous. Blizzards develop when a fierce wind whips up the snow, piling it in drifts while

other areas are swept clear. If there have been heavy falls of snow and the ensuing thaw is rapid, dangerous floods can occur.

(*Left*) an Alpine snowscape; (*above*) icicles in a Czech winter landscape. Ice and snow can shatter and erode the surface of the land. In past times, with different world climate patterns, ice sheets have covered large areas which today have a temperate climate, causing characteristic types of weathering.

Rivers of ice

Snowfields are created where snow lies undisturbed from year to year. Gradually the weight of the snow in the upper layers compresses that beneath, squeezing out air and water to make pellets of ice. Compacted together these have a granular texture. At this stage in glacier formation, the ice is called névé, and is about 30m (100ft) thick in an established valley glacier. At lower levels the pressure becomes even greater, and further compaction turns the névé into true blue-grey-coloured glacier ice.

Snow continues to accumulate, and with the increasing weight the pressure on the ice beneath forces it outwards from the collecting area. It moves down the valleys as great tongues of ice, called glaciers.

Such valley glaciers are well developed in central Asia, the Alps (*right*, Morteratsch Glacier, Switzerland; *above*, glaciers in the Breithorn area of the Alps) and the Andes. Alaska has some of the longest glaciers in the world.

The mechanism by which glaciers move is not fully understood, although the lower layers seem to be viscous while the upper ones are brittle. The brittleness of the upper layers of ice causes fractures and fissures, known as crevasses, to appear when the surface tension alters.

Floating islands

Today only 15.6 million sq km of the earth's surface is covered with ice, although of course this varies from year to year. The only ice-sheets are located in Greenland and Antarctica. The ice in these regions can be in excess of 3050m (10,000ft) thick. Smaller accumulations of ice, known as ice-caps, are found in Iceland,

Spitzbergen and on the Arctic islands.
Were all the ice in the world to melt, the sea
level would rise by about 61m (230ft), flooding
many areas, and drowning many important
parts of the earth.

When a glacier or ice-sheet reaches the sea, it
will spread outwards into it until the water is
deep enough to cause the ice to float. Large
masses then break away to become icebergs by
a process known as calving. Here are bergs
originating from Greenland (*far left*) and
the Arctic (*opposite*). About one-tenth of the
iceberg appears above the water.

The bergs drift on the currents, and can be a
serious hazard to shipping if they travel far
enough from the polar regions. The most
famous disaster involving such a collision was in
April 1912, when the liner *Titanic* sank on her
maiden voyage, with a loss of more than 1500
lives.

The Ross Ice Shelf, Antarctica, terminates in
ice cliffs in excess of 60m (200ft). It is from the
Antarctic ice that the largest of all bergs are
calved, the flat-topped tabular bergs which
average 30–50km (20–30m) in length, and can
have an area in excess of 33,000sq km.

(*Above*) is the inaccessible, hostile landscape
of the Brooks Range, Alaska. The glaciated
landscape and extremely low temperatures mean
that the population is minimal. In such areas of
Tundra, the subsoil is frozen for most or all of
the year, preventing the development of any
substantial vegetation.

The Dead Sea

The Dead Sea, on the borders of Israel and Jordan (*left* Israel; *below left* Jordan) is 79km (49m) long and varies between 5km (3m) and 16km (10m) in width. It is the lowest lake in the world, being 394m (1293ft) below the level of the Mediterranean Sea and having, at its maximum, a depth of about 397m (1304ft). The Dead Sea formed in a down-warp of the earth's crust which extends through the Middle East and down into Africa as the Great Rift Valley. Because of its low-lying situation rivers are able to flow into it, although the only major one is the Jordan – but there is no outlet whereby the water can escape.

The rivers bring in quantities of dissolved minerals and because of the high temperatures, and hence the evaporation of water, the Dead Sea is about five times as salty as the ocean. A salty residue is to be found around the shores, coating logs and drift-wood. It is impossible for a swimmer (*below right*) to sink in the water.

WONDERS IN THE AIR

Inside the Arctic and Antarctic circles, for example as here in Greenland, the sun does not set for days or even weeks and months. The 'Land of the Midnight Sun' is an apt name for the northern regions, and it is often applied to northern Norway where the sun is continuously above the horizon from 12th May until 29th July. At the poles the sun does not set for six months at a time. The reason for the midnight sun is that the axis of the earth is inclined at 23.5° to the perpendicular. If the axis was not inclined, the sun would always be over the equator and consequently there would be no seasons and no midnight sun.

Eclipse

Nothing can be more frightening than the obscuring of the sun by the moon during a total eclipse. However, such a dramatic event depends solely on the coincidence of the distances between earth, moon and sun, and on the size of the moon.

Astronomers make good use of a total eclipse (*below*) to study the two outer layers of the sun – the chromosphere and the corona.

At any one point on the earth's surface a total eclipse is relatively rare. On the right is an eclipse of the sun by the earth taken from space. The bright crescent above the earth is caused by the sun shining through the gases in the earth's atmosphere.

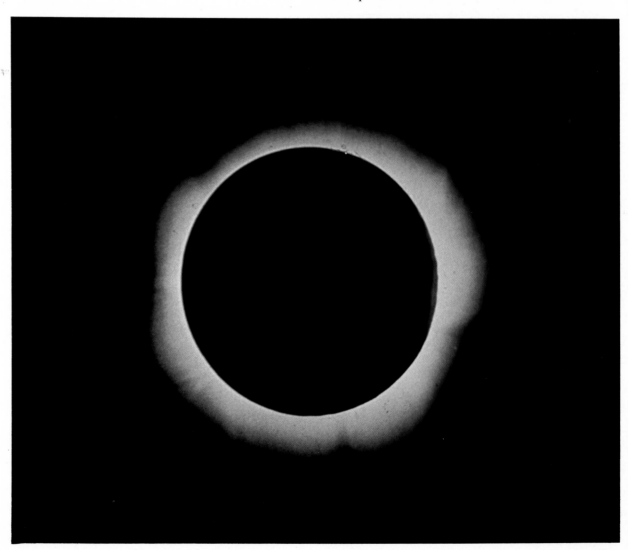

Thunder and lightning

Sound and light travel at different speeds, and consequently it is possible, by counting the seconds between the flash of lightning and the crash of thunder, to estimate how far away the storm is.

Clouds which form during the evolution of a thunderstorm are very turbulent and rise to considerable heights. For reasons not yet fully understood, the clouds develop an electrical field with a positive charge in the upper layers and a negative one lower down. The surface of the earth is normally negatively charged. Because of the negative charge in the base of the thunder cloud a 'shadow' positive charge is induced on the ground below. This charge attempts to flow upwards into the atmosphere, but because air is a poor conductor, a considerable difference between the two charges is necessary for a discharge.

The actual lightning evolves in a series of steps, or 'leaders', down from the clouds. Gradually the resistance of the air is overcome. When earth is reached a return stroke flashes up this prepared channel. Finally a sustained charge between earth and cloud is established.

Lightning does not always reach the ground, but sometimes discharges between cloud and cloud. Forked lightning (*below and left*) is branched.

Aerial illusions

The movie director's stand-by for the hero lost in the desert is the sighting of a mirage (*above left*: over the Sahara; *above right* over the stony desert in Algeria).

Under ordinary circumstances the human eye sees objects by means of the light rays reflected from them. Because such rays travel in a straight line it is usually possible to see only features which are above the horizon.

In the desert the density of the layers of air above the surface varies considerably. The air next to the sand is very light and hot, while that above is slightly colder and denser. This upper layer acts as a mirror. The light rays from an object – for example, an oasis or mountain chain – are reflected back to earth, and hence it appears on the horizon when in reality it is many miles away. According to the variation in the density of the layers a double image may form in which the bottom part is inverted.

Of all the atmospheric displays the rainbow (*right* over Luneberg Heath, Germany) is one of the most attractive. Rainbows are due to the refraction and reflection of the rays of the sun by millions of raindrops and hence are characteristic of showery weather. They display the colours of the spectrum, for the raindrops act as tiny prisms. When there is a double rainbow, the outer one is usually less brilliant.

54

Maverick winds

The tornado is the strongest and fiercest of all the many different types of wind. It is a violent destroyer of all in its path, but it does have a short life, and the path it follows is not usually very wide.

The wind in a tornado revolves in an anti-clockwise direction setting up a whirlwind effect. Such winds are associated with thunderstorms or humid weather. Indeed the word is derived from the Spanish *tornada*, meaning a thunderstorm. The most tornado-prone areas of the world are the central and eastern parts of the United States.

When a tornado forms over water it is called a waterspout (*above*). It appears as though an inverted cone is hanging from the dark cloud to connect with the water surface. A considerable quantity of water is gathered up into the swirling air, and in the centre of the spout there is heavy rain.

Related but much less violent are water-devils (*left*: Lake Ambrosia, Kenya), which start on land and then travel onto water where they die. Similar whirling winds over land are called land-devils, and are particularly common in the central states of the USA.

Even a light wind blowing over loose sand and dust will lift and carry some of the particles a short distance. In many arid areas the wind blows strongly without any barriers, and is capable of removing sand in vast clouds which darken the whole sky (*below* near Tenerife). Once into the air the dust and sand may be carried for many miles, and the red rain experienced over Italy and very occasionally in Britain is due to the sand from the Sahara. Other maverick winds include the cyclone. This is a particularly strong and violent revolving wind storm in the tropics. Such storms are a constant threat in such countries as Bangladesh. In the Caribbean they occur frequently, but are called hurricanes. In Japan and China such storms are known as typhoons; in western Australia as willy willies.

Cyclones are intense centres of low pressure. The centre, or eye, of the cyclone is particularly hazardous. Heavy, dark clouds build up and torrential rain follows.

WONDERS OF LIVING THINGS

Islands have a fascination all their own – particularly coral islands, such as these in the Fiji group, in the Pacific Ocean. The history of such islands is remarkable, for they are created by fiery volcanoes spurting out red-hot lava. When the lava finally stops and the volcano dies it gradually sinks beneath the waves of the ocean. While still active, however, the corals will already have started to grow around its submerged slopes, forming a fringing reef.

Wilderness life

Many members of the plant kingdom show striking adaptations to cope with the environment in which they grow, but the cactus group (*below*, spherical cacti from Mexico) is an example of quite an incredible transformation. Their leaves have been completely transformed into hairs and spines which protect them from the attentions of browsing animals. The lack of leaves also greatly reduces the water-loss through transpiration, and therefore helps the cactus to conserve water. To carry out the normal food-production processes in the absence of leaves, the cactus stem is green and adapted to this function. It is also equipped to store a considerable quantity of water. This is why they appear swollen and succulent. Because of their unique water storage facilities cacti can make the best use of the occasional downpour by quickly taking up vast quantities of moisture. The roots of the cactus plant usually penetrate deep into the soil, although some forms have a very shallow, but widespread, root system. Cacti are natives of the arid regions of North and South America, and vary in size from a few centimetres to well over 10m (33ft). The *Saguaro* cactus, the giant of the family, which has been known to reach 15m (50ft), is also one of the world's slowest-growing plants.

The record for the plant which takes the longest time to flower is, however, held not by a cactus but by a herb called *Puya raimondii*, which grows in the Peruvian Andes (*left*) and takes about 150 years to produce a flower. The flower cluster is itself a record-holder, reaching more than 10m (33ft) in height.

The tallest trees

Some of the mightiest of the world's living forms are found in the western United States. Trees come in all shapes and sizes, but there are very few that can compare with the Giant Sequoia (*Sequoiadendron giganteum*) (*below*). It is a conifer which reaches heights of over 80m (260ft). One particular tree, named 'General Sherman' (*right*) in the Sequoia National Park, California, is the world's largest living organism, standing 83m (272ft) tall and with a girth of just under 25m (82ft). It is estimated to weigh 2030 tonnes. These trees are only found growing naturally in the western Sierra Nevada of California, although they have been successfully grown in many countries including Britain, where they are called Wellingtonias. The age of some of the large specimens has been estimated to be between 3000 and 3500 years old.

The tallest trees also come from California, and are the Coast Redwoods (*Sequoia sempervirens*) which grow to more than 100m (328ft). The tallest at present is about 110m (360ft) high. The Sequoias are named after a Cherokee Indian chief, Sequoyah, who invented a phonetic alphabet in the nineteenth century.

INDEX

Page numbers in italics refer to illustrations

This edition published in 1980 by
Octopus Books Limited
59 Grosvenor Street, London W1

ISBN 0 7064 1122 6

© 1979 Octopus Books Limited

Produced by
Mandarin Publishers Limited
22a Westlands Road
Quarry Bay, Hong Kong

Printed in Hong Kong

PDO 79-472